Albino Animals

Marie Racanelli

PowerKiDS press

New York

To Jenny and Jessica

Published in 2010 by The Rosen Publishing Group, Inc.
29 East 21st Street, New York, NY 10010

First Edition

Editor: Joanne Randolph
Book Design: Greg Tucker
Photo Researcher: Jessica Gerweck

Photo Credits: Cover Gary Vestal/Getty Images; p. 5 © Steffen Schellhorn/age fotostock; pp. 7, 9, 15 Shutterstock.com; p. 11 © Chris Mattison/age fotostock; p. 12–13 © Alberto Carrera/age fotostock; p. 17 © Paco Elvira/age fotostock; p. 19 © R. Andrew Odum/Peter Arnold, Inc.; p. 21 © www.iStockphoto.com/Yang Lee.

Library of Congress Cataloging-in-Publication Data

Racanelli, Marie.
  Albino animals / Marie Racanelli. — 1st ed.
      p. cm. — (Crazy nature)
  Includes index.
  ISBN 978-1-4358-9381-8 (library binding) — ISBN 978-1-4358-9854-7 (pbk.) —
ISBN 978-1-4358-9855-4 (6-pack)
  1. Albinos and albinism—Juvenile literature. 2. Animals—Color—Juvenile literature. I. Title.
  RL790.R33 2010
  616.5'5—dc22
                                          2009034092

Manufactured in the United States of America

CPSIA Compliance Information: Batch #WW10PK: For Further Information contact Rosen Publishing, New York, New York at 1-800-237-9932

Contents

What Is Albinism?

The world is full of animals that come in a rainbow of colors. There are pink flamingos, green frogs, blue herons, orange and black tigers, and more. Sometimes, though, an animal may be born with different coloring from other animals like it. Some animals are born with white fur and pink eyes. These animals are albinos.

If a tree frog is born with albinism, how does it differ from a tree frog that is green? In most ways, the two frogs do not differ at all. They like the same foods. They are both about the same size. They even make the same sounds. The only difference is that the albino frog is missing a **pigment** called **melanin**.

Can you tell which of these minks is the albino? Minks, which are related to otters and weasels, are generally dark in color, like the one on the right.

Power of Pigment

Pigments are necessary in order to have the many colors we see in animals, humans, and nature. Leaves are green, and male cardinals are red because of pigments. Melanin is the pigment that produces colors in skin, hair, and eyes. Melanin can be brownish black or reddish yellow. Animals with albinism do not make melanin. When this pigment is missing in animals, it leads to the absence of color in their skin, hair, feathers, fur, **scales**, and eyes.

Animals cannot catch albinism from each other. They are born with it. It is in their **genes**. This means it is a **disorder** that is passed down from their parents.

Kangaroos generally have brown, gray, or reddish fur and live in hot, sunny Australia. Albino kangaroos can get badly sunburned in their habitat.

Not All White Animals Are Albinos

How do you know if a white animal is a true albino? You need to look at its eyes. The lack of melanin produces eyes that look pinkish red or blue. This is the eye color of a true albino. White animals that have regular coloring in their eyes are called **leucistic**. These animals have a reduction in all skin pigments, not just melanin.

Some animals, like the polar bear or snowy owl, have white fur or feathers, but they are not albino or leucistic. Their bodies produce pigments, but they have adapted, or changed over time, to having white coverings because it helps them live in their snow-covered homes.

Leucistic animals are not as uncommon as albinos, but you still do not see them often in the wild. Here you can see a leucistic peacock.

Not All Albinos Are White

Normally, the fur, feathers, or scales of albino animals are all white, and the eyes are pink or pale blue. In a few cases, these animals may begin to show some color as they grow older. This can happen if the animal produces very small amounts of melanin, if its body makes other pigments besides melanin, or if it gets pigments from its food. These animals are still called albinos because of their light-colored eyes and low melanin production.

Some albino animals, however, produce melanin in some parts of their bodies, such as their tails or their ear tips. These animals are considered to be partial albinos.

This albino gopher snake has yellow markings on its scales. This is because most snakes have other kinds of pigments besides melanin in their bodies.

Crazy Albino Facts!

1. Albino animals have pinkish red eyes.

2. Not everyone agrees about whether insects can be albinos since they do not have skin in the same way other animals do. They do have a form of melanin, though.

3. The chances of an albino lobster being born is 1 in 100 million.

4. There are likely only about 30 albino alligators alive in the world today. Most of them live in zoos.

5. When two parents carry the **recessive** gene that causes albinism, there is still only a one in four chance the baby will be born an albino.

6. Zookeepers in Australian zoos must put sunscreen on their albino kangaroos so they will not get sunburned.

7. One in twenty thousand people is born with albinism.

8. Even plants can grow white, but this is always deadly for them. If a plant lacks chlorophyll, which is a green chemical in its leaves that it needs to make food from sunlight, it cannot live once it uses up the stored food in its seed.

Albino Eyesight

All albino animals have poor eyesight. This is due to the lack of melanin in their eyes. Melanin helps the eyes develop normally. With little or no melanin, the eyes cannot develop the way a healthy animal's eyes will. While albinos are not totally blind, they cannot see very well.

Melanin also gives the eye's iris its color. When there is no melanin, blood vessels show through the iris. That is why the eyes of an albino animal usually appear to be pinkish red. Sometimes, light shining into the iris can make the eyes look very pale blue.

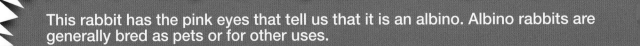

This rabbit has the pink eyes that tell us that it is an albino. Albino rabbits are generally bred as pets or for other uses.

All Creatures Great and Small

Albinism occurs in nearly every kind of animal species. It has been found in **mammals**, reptiles, amphibians, fish, birds, and shellfish. From snails to squirrels and from people to whales, albinism can be found all over the world.

People are often interested in seeing albino animals. Over the years, some of these animals have become well known. One famous albino animal was a gorilla named Snowflake. He was born in Africa. After he was caught, he lived for 40 years in Spain's Barcelona Zoo. Many people came to see Snowflake. The zookeepers and visitors to the zoo were sad when he died.

Snowflake looks quite different from his dark-colored neighbors shown here. Snowflake was found as a baby on Africa's west coast in 1967.

Challenges of Albinism

Many animals are **predators**. It is hard for albino animals to hide from these hunters. Their white bodies and poor eyesight make them easy to hunt. These things also make it hard for albino predators to hunt well. They cannot easily see their **prey**, and the prey can see them coming. Albino animals are also not picked as mates because they look so different.

Snakes, frogs, and alligators need sunlight to keep warm. This is a problem if they have albinism. Because they have no melanin, albino animals have **sensitive** skin and sunburn easily. The sun hurts them instead of warming them.

Most alligators and crocodiles are greenish or brownish to blend in with the places where they live. It will be hard for this alligator to sneak up on prey.

The Albino Squirrels of Olney, Illinois

Many people who live in Olney, Illinois, think their city is special. Do you know why? Olney is the home of about 200 albino squirrels. Each fall, people count the squirrels to see if their numbers have gone up or down. A festival is also held in their honor.

Special laws in Olney **protect** the squirrels. If a squirrel is in the street, cars have to stop so the squirrel can pass. Dogs and cats are not allowed to run loose because they can hurt the squirrels. To show their support, police officers in Olney even have an image of an albino squirrel on their arm patch.

Most squirrels count on their fur to blend in with the trees. The squirrels of Olney are lucky that they have people watching out for them!

Why Are Albino Animals So Rare?

Each parent must carry the recessive gene that causes albinism. If only one has it, then the animal will not be albino. The chances are small that two animals with this same gene will have babies together. That is why albinism, in general, is so rare.

When albinism does occur in the wild, the animals have a small chance of staying alive. They have a better chance in zoos, where people take care of them. The people who live in Olney, Illinois, protect their albino squirrels. If there were more places like Olney, then maybe other albino animals would also have a chance to live long lives.

Glossary

disorder (dis-OR-der) A sickness or medical condition.

genes (JEENZ) Tiny parts in the centers of cells. Genes tell your cells how your body will look and act.

leucistic (loo-KIS-tik) Having to do with a disorder in which the body does not make any pigments.

mammals (MA-mulz) Warm-blooded animals that have a backbone and hair, breathe air, and feed milk to their young.

melanin (MEH-luh-nun) The dark pigment that determines the color in skin, hair, fur, feathers, scales, and eyes.

pigment (PIG-ment) Matter that gives color.

predators (PREH-duh-terz) Animals that kill other animals for food.

prey (PRAY) An animal that is hunted by another animal for food.

protect (pruh-TEKT) To keep from being hurt.

recessive (rih-SEH-siv) Having to do with a gene that does not give traits unless there are two present.

scales (SKAYLZ) The thin, dry pieces of skin that form the outer covering of snakes, lizards, and other reptiles.

sensitive (SEN-sih-tiv) Easily hurt.

Index

A

albinism, 4, 6, 13, 16, 18, 22
albino(s), 4, 8, 10,13, 14, 16, 18, 20, 22

C

coloring, 4, 8
color(s), 4, 6, 8, 10, 14

D

disorder, 6

E

eyes, 4, 6, 8, 10, 13–14

F

food(s), 4, 10, 13
frog(s), 4, 18
fur, 4, 6, 8, 10

G

gene(s), 6, 13, 22

H

humans, 6

L

laws, 20
leaves, 6, 13

M

mammals, 16
melanin, 4, 6, 8, 10, 13–14, 18

P

parent(s), 6, 13, 22
pigment(s), 4, 6, 8, 10
predators, 18
prey, 18

S

scales, 6, 10
skin, 6, 8, 13, 18

Web Sites

Due to the changing nature of Internet links, PowerKids Press has developed an online list of Web sites related to the subject of this book. This site is updated regularly. Please use this link to access the list:

www.powerkidslinks.com/cnature/albino/